No Dad

Big Deal

Still I Rise

May God bless you in all that you do!!

Sam-Jay Robinson

No Dad Big Deal

No Dad Big Deal

Published by

Peaches

Publications

No Dad Big Deal

No Dad Big Deal

Published in London by Peaches Publications, 2019.

www.peachespublications.co.uk

British Library Cataloguing in Publication Data: A catalogue record for this book is available from the British Library.

ISBN: 9781712492079

Book cover design: Peaches Publications.

Typesetter: Winsome Duncan.

Proofreader and Editor: Laurelle Brant.

No Dad Big Deal

Contents

Dedication

To the fatherless.

Acknowledgements

I want to give a huge shoutout to my publisher Winsome Duncan for helping me through my life and aiding me on my journey to becoming an author.

I also want to bless Vinessa and Laurelle Brant for letting me work through this stage of my life and for putting up with my behaviour throughout this stressful time of transition. I must give a lot of credit to Auntie Mary Adeyeye because of all of the motivation her and Adewale Adeyeye (her husband) have given me throughout my years of me knowing them. I want to thank all of the men in my life for being that father figure that I haven't had in 6 years:

1. David Parkinson -church brother who always speaks and helps me if there is an issue at home.

2. James Summut -football coach who has always encouraged me to strive.

3. Gershom J Allen (Dr G) -the best motivational speaker that has ever spoken to me and helped me to overcome my problems.

4. Uncle Ev and Auntie Karen Robinson - my very own Uncle and Auntie who has never looked down on me and has always been there to talk to, (even abroad) just regularly checking up on all of us at home.

5. Flight Lieutenant Terry McCarty RAFAC - my RAF Air Cadets Officer Commanding for also encouraging me to go for higher levels in the RAF (promotion, sports competitions and helping me to do well representing London Wing).

6. Pastor Matthew Ashimolowo: My Pastor, who has shown us all that Abba Father can turn my mess into a message; how a test has become my testimony! He has always given me a sense of worth and the feeling that I am, in fact, something special to him and to God.

Introduction

No dad is, in fact, a big deal. See, without a father, you have the 'key' man missing from your family and it is hard to step up into his position as a child. It tends to almost feel like your young life has ended due to your dad's absence.

As a matter of fact, it is scientifically proven that there are a lot of problems with children that grow up from a young age without a dad (like many people in the world, including myself).

As cited at https://owlcation.com/social-sciences/Psychological-Effects-On-Men-Growing-Up-Without-A-Father

Young people without a father or father-figure display the following traits; They are...

1. More likely to be aggressive
2. More likely to be depressed
3. More likely to have a low self-esteem

4. More likely to do poorly in school
5. More likely to be incarcerated and to commit suicide
6. More likely to take drugs.

However, not having a dad is not necessarily the worst outcome thinkable, particularly if they refused to love the families they created by leaving their homes in the first place. Whatever the reason, including death, this difficult journey (if you travel right), will equip you to become stronger and help you form into that destined locked up adult inside you. A tragic event like this can help you to overcome your worst fears and failures, moulding you into a better role model for the future.

> **"I first felt that having no dad would be the end of me. However, various strategies have helped me to become a stronger man, helping me to become more**

confident in sharing and empowering more like-minded individuals in this challenging journey. I am not at all saying it's good to not have a dad, but to have key things in place for me, has just made me stronger."

Sam-Jay Robinson

This book is a collection of my blog entries which was split into four sections and covered the poignant stages of my journey:

Finding Out - This part of the book is about "Finding Out" that your dad is playing away or he may be on his way to glory. (The moment you realised that your home isn't a happy home.)

He's Gone - This part of the book is after you find out about your dad's situation. Now he has left your life and you are left with your mother and siblings if you have any- (The moment he is physically not in your life)

What's Next? - This is about the future of your life and how you cope with this situation. What has God got in-store for you? (The atmosphere has changed, what is going on?)

Came Through- This is about your life and how you can still be successful despite what has happened (you will still rise).

You are not alone. Let's walk through this journey together, we have no choice but to make it!

Chapter 1

Hole Hearted to Whole Hearted

Finding Out

I am here to let you know that it is not your father that is in disbelief, you are. Most of the time children, teenagers and young adults are complaining about their failures and are putting it to the fact that they don't have a dad. Guys, please. Let me tell you something, remember this (if you forget anything else): you don't need a dad, you need a Father. A father is the one who really helps you in being successful and to achieve all round excellence with your Sport or Arts (Music, Drama and Dance), social skills and not forgetting also being good at your studies and homework at school or college. Your dad is just the one who procreated you.

A father is someone who plays a greater role than that.

Yes, I thought that it was the school or class bully that had no dad around and this is why they had to take their hurt out on us all. Oh, how I was clearly wrong.

However in 2014, life at home took an unfavourable turn. My dad would come home at 2200 hrs from work and he would say that he was talking to his friends (he didn't have any friends!!!) or he worked over time (which never happens in all of my 10 years of living). Then in January 2015, my dad deserted me and my family by a text message sent to my Mother. I checked under our stairs cupboard and saw that his coats and shoes were gone. But I was never, I am not, and never planned to be a school or class bully so why is this happening to me?

Of course, this is to the fatherless boys and girls (fathers who have passed away), whom are very much welcome too. I'm just being me, giving tips on how to cope and how I cope by talking about boy things such as Football, LEGO and much more. More importantly how you to become the man or, in general, the head of the house. Not forgetting to give out all the inspirational quotes that have got me through the tough times.

"Yes, Dad is gone but look, we can all still make it!"

Chapter 2

How to help myself by making things worse

I'm pretty sure that we would never dishonour our dads when they were with us. Well, I certainly wouldn't, but I had to on this occasion. In one of my blogs, it speaks about when I was playing a football game on my dad's phone that I really liked and I accidentally clicked on the text message notification. It showed me all of his texts (some appropriate but mostly inappropriate). Anyway, this is based on me helping myself by basically "snitching" on my dad because I knew that I couldn't live the rest of my life with an unhappy family. With a dad like that, who I know is cheating on my mother and him lying to us all, not knowing that his son knows the whole story and knows the real reason why he is always late home- I was simply unable to keep it in any longer.

With all of these negative feelings and no-one to take it away from me, I knew that only I could help myself. But, whatever I chose to do, it could or will make things worse. Really, in a situation like this, there are two pathways.

1.   Keeping quiet – however, in my situation, I would be just as bad as my dad by keeping this horrible secret. It was getting annoying and stressful because every time I was playing my game on his phone and she would break into my family home with her "strange" messages, it would constantly come up so I was constantly swiping them away and messages continued even when I had to come off his phone. I often only played 1 match, equating to about 3 minutes- which meant that most of my

down-time was stressful and filled by getting rid of the evidence of my dad's mistress.

2.   Telling your other, and loyal, parent (in this case, my mother) – There will definitely be a reaction from them; who wouldn't react to the news that their long-term partner is seeing someone else?! But anything is better than keeping quiet. Suffering in secret really hurts and it made me so grouchy, scared and tired.

So I clearly went for option 2, I helped myself get rid of all of the stress of knowing something that I didn't want ever to happen or know. It wasn't fair because this had nothing to do with me but it was involving the most important person to me. Things would be worse for my mother, my dad or myself but at least I wouldn't be alone.

"Suffering in secret really does hurt."

Chapter 3

Had to learn to ignore the ignorable

He has gone

Around 2014, Christmas time, my dad walked out on us. He left myself and 2 young, beautiful and smart ladies and our family home for a "high school" friend. Pretty disgraceful but I have had to live with it for 3 years.

I am a teenager and my dad still has the cheek to ask if he can see my sister and myself. My dad still hasn't admitted to what he has done.

The fact is that I had to find out for myself, whilst I was in the middle of a football game that was on his phone. Then a notification appeared that came from a lady that I had never heard of in my life. But I accidentally tapped on it and I saw all of their texts to each other. I told my mother and that was history, yet he still is asking to this day to see my sister and I; albeit not my Mother. My dad hasn't come home since then.

Looking back, I didn't explain totally to my mum what was going on. I told her that weird stuff was coming up on dad's phone (for instance: xx, what hotel are we staying in, love you...). My mother told me to forget all of it and come away from my dads phone. NO WAY!!! I love "Dream League Soccer" but I told myself that I would ignore the notifications because it wasn't for me anyway.

But I remember, not long afterwards, my mum asked me for my dad's phone password. Life changed for the worse yet better. Worse- as he went around the house like a big, angry animal rather than a dad. Better because he left us alone and stopped trying too hard to be nice to me and not to my Mother and my sister and talking to them like a stranger, which protected us all in the long-term.

Looking further back, I think my Mother told me to ignore the messages so that I didn't focus on what my dad was up to. But, really, I know I gave her a reason to find out the truth on her own. Adult stuff I guess.

"Life could be hard at the beginning but it will become easier as you get older and more successful."

IGNORE IT

Chapter 4

Fear isn't a place where you come from

I have spoken about the way that I enjoy sports and especially football and athletics. The recent football event (The FIFA World Cup) was a great event and the countries that played were very committed. I watched nearly every single match since I was so happy about having the opportunity to see it. My Mother, Sister and I watched England get to the semi-finals (and lost, sadly). But, what was so much sadder than anything else: not having my whole family, the 4 of us not, watching it. My dad wasn't there to cheer with us, only 3 out of 4 were happy.

Yes, I was upset but I didn't let one main part in my life not let me have a great World Cup season. Raheem Sterling, the left striker, spoke about fear and about his father's death before one of the first World Cup Group Stages and, even though he remembered his father during the World Cup, he didn't let that stop him from playing well. Even though he made some mistakes throughout the big event that other people didn't like, he still played well in our eyes and that's what matters. Despite what he'd been through, he is a very successful role model and an exemplar of what we can all achieve.

F.E.A.R.

F =False

E = Evidence

A = Appearing

R = Real

Chapter 5

Life and living

To this day, my family and I are still barely surviving and my mothers work isn't helping the situation at all. My mum had recently been made redundant and now she has no job. The headteacher of the school is, technically, my mother's boss and my mum was a CSW, helping deaf children by signing to them. She is a Level 6, which is the highest level attainable, and her boss made her redundant for a Level 3 signer who is her "mate". Anyway, my mum has now got a part-time BSL-communication job in a university.

But we are still struggling, so we just pray to God and He has answered our prayers. We are still surviving, and that is the main feat, and we are still being fed. We have to be grateful for having the things we have now because there are some people who don't have what we have and what I have.

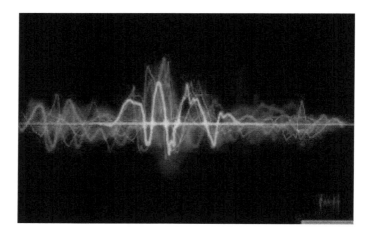

"Always be grateful for what you have because God can easily give it away."

Chapter 6

Contact

Recently, I had a thought. I remembered the last time I spoke to my dad, which was in Year 5, and now I am in Year 10 and, still, my mother is still waiting for him to sign the divorce papers. He has still left the garden in a mess (which we cannot deal with) and my mum is still in debt. We rely on food banks which our church provides.

Whilst struggling, I contacted my dad in desperation for something that I needed. He picked up and was shocked to hear my voice and how I sounded different. We spoke for a bit and spoke about how the family was. I eventually got to the point of why I contacted him and he made me a deal, he said "I will get you what you want if you ask your mother to stay in contact with me." So I asked my mother and she was quite upset because she explained how she had done everything she could to protect my sister and I from him, as he used to shout at my mother and my sister but not to me. My mother got upset and I tried everything I could to help her but she didn't seem to listen and I don't know why.

Later that day, my mother and I went out shopping and we spoke about the reason why I made that phone call. She explained why she was disappointed, stating that she had expected me to be the man of the house by now, however, I had only proven that I wasn't ready because as I still called him to help me when he was completely out of our lives. From then, I understood why she was so upset with me, and I apologized and we hugged it out and carried on with our day.

My dad made the deal with me so that he could speak to me and not my sister. A few months ago, he found out what school my sister went to and he asked her what she wanted. She asked for a new phone and he got it for her, but he kept on calling her over time, especially when she was working so she couldn't always pick up but he was getting annoyed with her. He called her again, she picked up and he had a go at her for not answering the phone, she explained herself. Eventually, he had had enough, he cut off the phone and tried to hack her phone but she blocked everything on it. He then got even more annoyed and upset and told me that he was happy with the fact that he was contacting me, and only me.

"I have learnt that I don't need anyone else to help me help my family and that 'I can do all things through Christ who strengthens me'."

Chapter 7

Majestic music

What Next?

The instruments that I play are the drums, guitar and the piano. Usually, I have a sort of emotion for each instrument. For instance, I play drums when I am angry or annoyed at something whereas I play the piano for comfort and to soothe myself. So, if you have and play an instrument, it'll be interesting to know what you use it for and, if you don't play an instrument, pick one up now!!!

I know some of you must be asking: What if I don't have an instrument? All you need to do is maybe pat a beat on your pillow or on your chair. And if you have the chance you can listen to some positive, upbeat music and make a good beat to it.

Yet, still, there is a common misconception that you have to be a musician to play music.

When people say that it really infuriates and upsets me, as it makes me feel as if you are saying to yourself that "I'm not sure if I am able to do this" and you are saying that you don't believe in yourself. Remember, you can do whatever you want to do, even if you have doubts in your heart because your world has just been turned upside down. As a child, we don't have control over everything but a powerful thing you can control is your music. This is a great way of relieving stress and increase creativity.

"It has been scientifically proven that creating music is good for you. So come on, make a joyful noise!!"

Chapter 8

Sports and leisure

This chapter generally talks about my life in sporting terms. I am a very sporty boy and I enjoy a lot of contact and non-contact sports such as: Rugby, Football, Basketball, Tennis, Cricket, etc. I also enjoy athletics. I love athletics, especially, as it is a very interactive activity. I am especially talented in long distance running such as 200m- 1800m. People say that I am really good at football and athletics but, personally, I'll say that I am not the best though.

I have taken part in many fitness activities such as the Essex Cross-Country Championships, representing Redbridge. I have taken part in the London Mini Marathon where you run past Buckingham Palace. I have started going to the gym a lot with my sister and mother and we go swimming in the morning before school every day at around 6:00am -7:45am. Ever since I started attending athletics clubs and training sessions, I have been getting through many competitions and, even though it is hard and sometimes I feel like I want to quit, I have got so far that there is no point in me quitting because all credit that I would have obtained would be gone!

When I participated in the Essex Cross-Country Championships, arguably the hardest competition I've ever competed in, half way through the race, I felt like I wanted to stop running and start walking. See, however, I knew that if I started to walk that I wouldn't be able to get back up again because I would be so comfortable to keep walking and I would come last. So I kept running and I, eventually, didn't finish last.

Even though I finished, I said told my mum that I want to quit running forever but I realised what is the real point of quitting. Since then, I've been participating in 'Park Runs' every Saturday and I still represent my school for Cross-Country and the borough of Redbridge for the London Mini Marathon.

Just remember, don't let little issues bring you down.

"It isn't over until you win!"

Les Brown

Chapter 9

Promotion

Came Through

As you know, I'm in the RAF Air Cadets and I've gone through a very tough time with my squadron. This issue occurred around February 2019. With my squadron, there have been many new staff members that join and try to make the squadron better for the public. So, there were 2 new staff members that joined and they came from another unit close to ours. Yet, one of the new members started off on a good note so that all of the cadets would enjoys their presence whereas the other new staff member had more of a stern personality and would be harsh and be more of a discipline-driven individual.

The RAF create opportunities for other squadrons to get together and do a camp.

What I noticed is that as soon as my mates and I signed up, the more curt staff member would sign up as well. There were a few instances when I felt a little targeted whilst I was with my friends in regards to my behaviour- even though I'm naturally a fun fellow! But, what I realised was that some people are placed into your life to test you- but I had to look over that and focus on my journey in the RAF.

Well, I got promoted to Corporal and on that day there were numerous responses from those in my squadron; some were red- faced and others were beaming. So my message is, don't let other men ruin your destiny and once you succeed in your career, that'll be a slap in the face to your enemies and that's what you want.

"Don't let others ruin your destiny."

Chapter 10

Being grateful

It was a very special occasion at this time. It was Christmas and yet we still rejoice and celebrate at Church and with family. But, on the down side of things, a long time may have passed without having our dads. My dad has been gone for 6 years and yes he still sends me birthday cards and money but not to my mother and sister though. It was my sister's 16th birthday and she didn't hear not one thing from my dad's side of the family.

I find that this is pretty unfair because I always get money and I always got what I wanted (when he was here), such as:

- Football Boots
- Footballs
- Football Shirts
- Trainers
- Games etc

But same as always, we are still coping. Surviving on food banks and people not paying my Mum her money, but we still strive for success because we still remember that there are the people that sleep outside and suffer day after day and we thank God for the opportunity of having a house of our own.

Epilogue

In all fairness, I have never spoken openly about how I feel towards the idea of my dad leaving me, yet the only outlet for me was to write a blog 3 years after the event happened. However, in writing this book, I have opened a few deep wounds, triggering a lot of emotions such as anger and frustration. I had decided and still working on putting all of my pain and hatred aside and focus on creating a brand new and better person (I am grateful for that). However, this is still the 1st time that I have openly spoken about the loss of my father, I am fully aware that the pain was shared through my close-knit family; creating an extremely difficult teenage boy. Yet, no child is going to come out of this mentally unharmed and it is difficult when you don't have two parents but with the right guidance, and with perseverance, we can get through this.

Now that you've read this book, I truly hope that it has showed you about all of the opportunities you can still have without having the 'main man' in your life. I thank you for reading this book and may God help you through all the steps in your life. Don't let that unfortunate moment drag you down; The 'Big Man' upstairs STILL has something in-store for you.

Keep your head up because there is no limit to your success and we both know that not even the sky is the limit.

Stay strong

Sam-Jay Robinson

About the Author

I am a 15-year-old young man and am gradually going the journey of my GCSE's. I participate in many activities outside school and book writing, such as:

-Cadets -recently promoted to Corporal

-Football -play LB for my local club

-Athletics -200m to 1500m runner for all athletics events (that I take part in). Won Jack Petchey award for my 800m enabling London represent South of England against North of England in the National Inter Wing Athletics competition.

-Cross Country -Participating in these events truly opened up many opportunities for me, allowing me to take part in the Virgin Money Giving Mini London Marathon (2nd time, debut in 2017 as a last-minute stand in U15 whilst still U13).

I've been doing blogs also and this is where my book was birthed from:

www.nodadbigdealblog.wordpress.com

www.samjayrobinson.weebly.com

As you know, this blog page talks about all of the trials and tribulations I have been through and, yet, I still can move forward and so should you.

WE PUBLISH
BOOKS

PEACHES

PUBLICATIONS

We Will Help You:
- Tell Your Story
- Become an Author
- Save You Time Writing

Our Services

Accountability Book Coaching
Silver Elite - Author's Starter Kit
Express Elite – Publish A Book In 4 Weeks
Gold Elite - Become A Publisher

Printed in Poland
by Amazon Fulfillment
Poland Sp. z o.o., Wrocław

61861826R00035